Dear _____,
your name

you are Beautiful no matter what they say! Here are a few things you should say everyday...

I AM SMART

I AM CONFIDENT

I
AM
BLACK

WE MATTER.

I AM BLESSED

I AM FRIENDLY

I AM GRATEFUL

I AM STRONG

I AM BRAVE

I AM UNSTOPPABLE

I
AM
THE FUTURE

Speak these words and don't back down, SMILE little black girl and fix your crown!

DEAR LITTLE BLACK GIRL

Dedicated to all the little black girls across the world

Made in the USA
Columbia, SC
13 January 2021